Computers

@ @ @

Don McLeese

ROURKE PUBLISHING

Vero Beach, Florida 32964

www.rourkepublishing.com

PHOTO CREDITS: © Yvonne Chamberlain: Title Page; © Rob Marmion: page 4; © AM29: page 5; Danny E. Hooks: page 6; © Thorpe: page 7; © Matt Gibbs (wikipedia.com): page 8; © The Supe87: page 9; © Phillipe de Champaigne: page 10 top; © David Monniaux (wikipedia.com): page 10 bottom; © Williv: page 11; © Henri Claudet: page 12 top, 44 top; © Andrew Dunn: page 12 bottom; © Bonnie Schupp: page 13, 44 middle; © Computer Labratory, University of Cambridge: page 14; © Fernando Blanco Calzado: page 15 left; © Jens Stolt: page 15 right; © Epolk: page 16; © Marc Dietrich: page 17; © Jacom Stephens: page 18; © Margot Petrowski: page 19; © Gaspare Messina: page 20; © National Semi-Conductor: 21 top; © Oktay Ortakcioglu: page 21 bottom, 45 top; © Microsoft: page 22, 23, 29, 45 middle; © Apple: page 24, 25, 28, 32, 38, 43; © Heidi Kristensen: page 26; © Microsoft Vista: page 27; © Sega: page 29 bottom; © Tulay Over: page 30; © Simon Podgorsek: page 31; © Terekhov Igor: page 33; © Blackred: page 34 top; © Grigory Bibikov: page 34 bottom; © Gabyjalbert: page 35; © Brandon Seidel: page 36; © Emrah Turudu: page 37; © Edward Andras: page 39; © Diego Cervo: page 40, 45 bottom; © Andrew Howe: page 41; © Paul Kline: page 42

Editor: Nancy Harris

Cover Design by Nicky Stratford, bdpublishing.com

Interior Design by Renee Brady

Library of Congress Cataloging-in-Publication Data

McLeese, Don.
  Computers / Donald McLeese.
     p. cm. -- (Let's explore technology communications)
  Includes index.
  ISBN 978-1-60472-329-8 (Hard cover)
  ISBN 978-1-60694-995-5 (Soft cover)
  1. Electronic digital computers--Juvenile literature. I. Title.
  QA76.52.M42 2009
  004--dc22

                                    2008019701

Rourke Publishing
Printed in China, Power Printing Company Ltd, Guangdong Province
101909
101909LS

www.rourkepublishing.com - rourke@rourkepublishing.com
Post Office Box 643328 Vero Beach, Florida 32964

Contents

CHAPTER ONE

A World Without Computers

Can you imagine a world without computers? Many of us play games on computers. We need them to send **email** or instant messages to our friends. We use them for our homework, to type papers, and to look for information.

We listen to music, watch movie DVDs, and keep photographs of our family and friends on computers. Many people shop for things using a computer. Some of us even write books on computers.

In 2007, with approximately 230.4 million personal computers in use, the United States had more personal computers in use than any other country.

We rely on computers for so much that it's nearly impossible to imagine life without them. However, it was not that long ago that there were no computers in our homes, our schools, or our libraries.

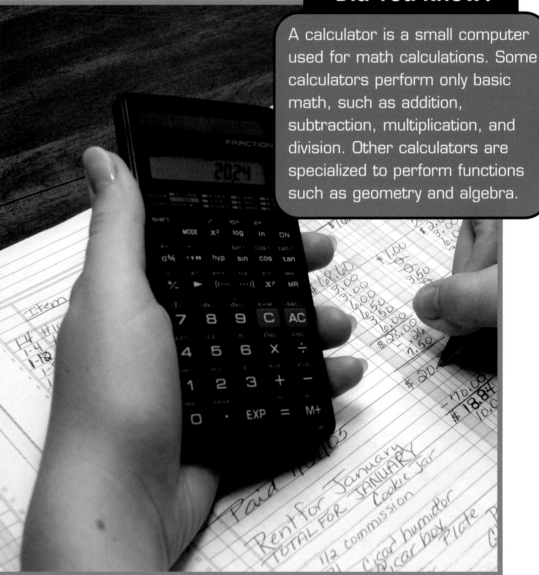

Did You Know?

A calculator is a small computer used for math calculations. Some calculators perform only basic math, such as addition, subtraction, multiplication, and division. Other calculators are specialized to perform functions such as geometry and algebra.

Before the mid-1970s, only big businesses and the government owned computers. The computers themselves were big—as big as a room, sometimes even as large as a house! Not only were they big, but they were so expensive that a household family wouldn't think of buying one. Computers cost millions of dollars and most people did not know what they would do with one if they had one. Now computers have changed our lives so much that we don't know what we would do without them.

CHAPTER TWO

What Is a Computer?

The word computer comes from compute, which means to add or subtract, like arithmetic. On the most basic level, a computer is a machine that computes. However, we now know that a computer can do so much more.

Everything that a computer does has to do with numbers. It transforms numbers into words, into pictures, and into sounds. It does these things much faster than a person ever could, even though everything that a computer does has been designed, or programmed, by a human being. A computer programmer is a person who knows how to write in a language that computers can understand.

Microprocessor

Computers are sometimes called **digital** computers. Digits are another word for numbers. The only digits that the computer understands are 1 and 0. The secret to computers is their ability to perform the most difficult tasks using these two simple digits. The code, or language, that computers understand is called **binary**. Bi- means two, so binary refers to the two digits that a digital computer uses.

CHAPTER THREE

Early Computers

Did you know that the first computers were invented in the 1600s, and that they were not run by **electricity**? A French mathematician named Blaise Pascal invented the first machine that could perform addition and subtraction, and it used wheels and gears to do so.

Prior to the mechanical ability to perform addition and subtraction, much of the world used the abacus. There are regions around the world where calculations are still performed using an abacus. Most of us simply use a calculator, one of today's simplest forms of a computer.

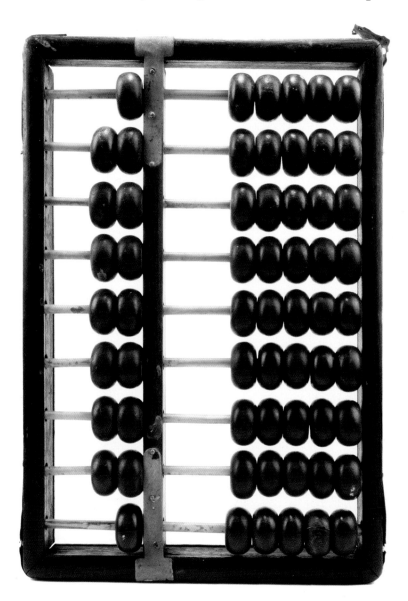

The science of computers made a big leap in the early 1800s, when an English mathematics professor named Charles Babbage advanced the wheel and gear system. Babbage is credited with inventing the first mechanical computer. Today's researchers have proven that given enough money his designs in the 1820s would have worked.

Babbage's computers operated like large clocks. Babbage added cards with holes punched in them, called punch cards, that stored information on what the machine had already computed. This gave the machine a **memory**. We still say that a computer has a memory. However, machines can't really remember anything at all. They save information on **hard drives** and computer chips.

In the 1960s, punch cards were the main way computer data was stored. By the late 1980s, punch cards were no longer in use.

CHAPTER FOUR
Computers Go Electric

Through the first half of the 1900s, computers continued to get better with the use of **electricity**. As electricity took the place of wheels and gears, computers eventually became faster, cheaper, and smaller. Yet the first electric computers could be the size of a small house!

American mathematician John V. Atanasoff developed the first electronic computer in 1939. By the 1950s, **transistors** enabled engineers to develop smaller and faster computers. The transistor replaced the larger vacuum tubes used by earlier computers. It also used less electricity and was about the size of a bean. The smaller computers that the transistor made possible were even more powerful.

Vacuum Tube

Transistor

Many companies and the government started using computers more frequently in the 1960s. They usually had computers the size of a room. These large computers were known as the **mainframe**.

Did You Know?

Today NASA (National Aeronautics and Space Administration) Ames Research Center in Silicon Valley, California is the site of the NASA Advanced Supercomputer (NAS) facility. It houses one of the most powerful supercomputers in the world. The SGI Altix ICE supercomputer system has a system memory of 20,800 gigabytes (GB). That's about the same amount of memory as 10,000 desktop PCs.

Smaller computers on desks then sent information into the mainframe, which stored information in its memory and performed calculations. The problem with this is that when the mainframe broke down or **crashed**, the smaller computers would not work until the mainframe was fixed.

CHAPTER FIVE

Personal Computers

The age of the personal computer began in the mid-1970s, with the development of the integrated circuit, or **silicon chip**. They could do what previously needed hundreds of transistors. The silicon chips continue to get smaller.

Silicon Valley

An area along the California coast south of San Francisco has become known as Silicon Valley, because of all the companies making silicon chips and other parts for computers that are based there. People think of Silicon Valley and computers the same way they think of Hollywood and movies, because so many people who work in the research and development of computer technology live there.

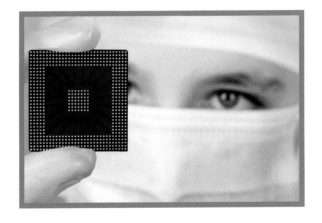

As technology advanced, many companies replaced mainframe computers with networked personal computers.

Did You Know?

Without personal computers, the Internet would not be what it is today. In 2007, the top ten countries for in-home internet usage were:

1. United States
2. China
3. Japan
4. Germany
5. India
6. United Kingdom
7. Korea
8. Brazil
9. France
10. Italy

Most of the computers we now use are personal computers. Desktop personal computers are not easy to move from place to place because they have several different parts. A desktop computers screen, keyboard, mouse, and central processing unit (CPU) are usually connected with wires. One advantage of desktop computers is that they are easier to upgrade than laptop computers.

Laptop computers are smaller and much easier to carry around. Both are complete computers that don't require a bigger mainframe for storing information.

Be careful with your laptop! Most laptop computer monitors are a liquid crystal display (LCD). LCDs are fragile and easy to damage. The only way to repair damaged LCD screens is to replace them. Depending on your laptop, a new screen may cost as much as your computer did.

CHAPTER SIX

Microsoft and Apple

Two companies that got their start in the mid-1970s continue to be leaders in the computer industry today. In 1975, two friends named Bill Gates and Paul Allen started a company called Microsoft. It later developed a system called Windows, which lets the computer do many different things at once. A computer that uses the Microsoft Windows technology is called a PC (personal computer).

The early slogan of Bill Gates was, "a computer in every home and on every desktop." Microsoft began reaching that goal when its operating system was used in IBM's 5150, the first popular computer designed for use by the general public.

Bill Gates was born on October 28, 1955. When he was 13, he wrote his first computer program. It was a tic-tac-toe game that people played against the computer.

The next year, two friends named Steve Jobs and Steve Wozniak started Apple Computers. Apple uses a different kind of technology from Windows. Personal computers are either PC or Apple, depending on whether they use the Microsoft operating system or are made by Apple.

Apple Desktop Computer

There have been many popular products designed by Apple. Some of them are the Macintosh computer, the iPod personal music player, and the iPhone.

iPod

iPhone

CHAPTER SEVEN

Hardware and Software

When we talk about computer hardware, we do not mean a hammer and nails or other things you can buy at a hardware store. Hardware is the computer itself and everything that is inside of it. The chips, the **keyboard**, and the other parts are all considered hardware.

Software refers to the various programs that the computer can run and the things that it can do. You must have software programs installed in your computer in order to play games, to type papers, to create art, or to do math problems.

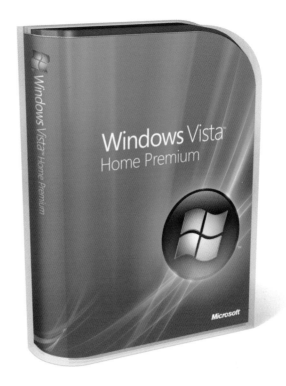

A big difference between Apple and Microsoft is that Apple makes software that can only run on Apple computers. Microsoft does not make computers. Instead, it designs software for use in almost all computers, including some that can run in Apple computers. It also created and is continuously updating an operating system called Windows.

When you buy a computer game or some other kind of software, you must make sure to purchase the Apple or the PC version, depending on what kind of a computer you have.

If you think kids play more video games and computer games than adults do, you're wrong. The average age of game players is 33 years old.

CHAPTER EIGHT

Parts of the Computer

Computers have many parts. Some of them we can see. Some of them are inside the computer, so we can't see them without taking the computer apart. Some parts are so small that we might not be able to see them at all.

The hard drive is where the computer stores most of its information. It lets the programs run and saves everything we want to keep in our computer, including all the songs, photos, and information we have typed. The hard drive is located inside the body of the computer.

A computer **monitor** is the screen where we see the work we are doing or game we are playing. Though the language of a computer is binary code (a series of 1's and 0's), the computer transformsthis code on the monitor into a language or pictures that we can understand.

If we're typing a document or an email, we use the keyboard. The arrow or **cursor** on the computer screen can be controlled by the **mouse**. A keyboard or mouse can be attached or wireless. You can use the mouse to control what you do and to complete tasks on the computer. For example in this book, some of the words were changed to dark, bold print using the mouse.

A **CD-ROM** (compact disc-read only memory) drive lets you listen to music or watch movies on **discs**. It can also be used to install software onto your computer, including computer games.

Your computer can store its memory on chips, which have millions of switches that control the flow of signals. They allow your computer to store codes or language that it wants to keep. Without memory, your computer would lose all its information every time you turned it off.

The central processing unit (**CPU**) is a chip that is small, but a very important part of your computer. It processes information quickly from the computer's memory, using the computer's program and operating system. It works with two kinds of memory: **RAM** (random access memory), which can change whenever you type something or save something else using software, and **ROM** (read only memory), which is read only and can't be changed. When you put a movie DVD into your **CD-ROM**, your CPU lets you play it, but not change it

The **modem** can be either inside or outside your computer. It lets you connect to the **Internet**, where you can visit **websites** and send emails or instant messages to others who have computers.

What Is a Router?

Many people use a router to connect the personal computers in their house together and to access the internet. Routers are devices that transfer data from one computer to another. Because of wireless technology, it's very important to have a password on your router. Otherwise, people outside your house or apartment might access your computer or the internet through your router.

CHAPTER NINE

Better and Better

Computers have gotten smaller, most of them have gotten less expensive, and almost all of them are faster with more memory. Every year, computers keep getting better and better.

Computers still use the same language, the binary code of 0s and 1s. They read these through electricity. A 1 means the electronic pulse is on. A 0 means it is off. It is the complex combination of pulses that are on and off that we experience as language, sound, and pictures. Each one of those 0s and 1s is called a **bit** (binary digit). A group of those bits that the computer turns into a letter or a number that we can read is called a **byte**.

Measurements of Memory

A **kilobyte** (KB) is about a thousand bytes. A **megabyte** (MB) is about a million bytes. A computer game might require many MBs of memory. A **gigabyte** (GB) is about a billion bytes of memory.

The more memory a computer has and the better its processor or central processing unit, the faster it can turn millions of bytes into a game we can play or a song we can hear.

CHAPTER TEN

Crash or Freeze

Have you ever had a computer quit working while you are in the middle of using it? When a computer screen goes blank, we call this a crash. A freeze occurs when the computer will no longer let you point and click with a mouse, the arrow just will not move, or you cannot type letters on the keyboard.

If your computer crashes or freezes, you can sometimes turn it off and restart or **reboot** it. Sometimes a computer repair person can either start it again or transfer what was on your computer's hard drive to a new computer.

CHAPTER ELEVEN

The Future for Computers

Computers have already changed our lives in so many different ways. For most of us, we would be lost without one. We shop, communicate, and learn on computers. Computers keep our most private information as well as our favorite songs.

Today we can own a computer that is as small as the smallest telephone. We can communicate with people from all over the world in an instant, find a satellite image of our own home, and watch the latest TV shows. How much will computers be able to do in the future? No matter what we can imagine, it might come true, and maybe even sooner than we can believe.

Timeline

1642: French scientist Blaise Pascal invents first machine that can solve addition and subtraction equations.

1832: English mathematician Charles Babbage adds punch cards that give the computer memory.

1939: American mathematician John V. Atanasoff develops the first computer powered by electricity.

1960s: Companies and the government start making more and more use of big computers.

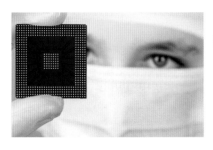

 1975: The development of the silicon chip made smaller computers possible. Bill Gates and Paul Allen start Microsoft.

 1976: Steve Jobs and Steve Wozniak start Apple Computers.

 1977: Apple begins selling its first popular computer, the Apple II.

 1981: IBM releases the popular 5150, using Microsoft's operating system.

 1984: Apple introduces its popular Macintosh computer.

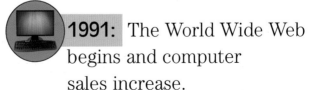 **1991:** The World Wide Web begins and computer sales increase.

Glossary

bit (bit): a single binary digit, a 1 or 0

byte (bite): a group of binary digits that a computer transforms into a number, letter, or something else

CD-ROM (SEE-DEE ROM): a computer drive that plays compact discs and has read-only memory

central processing unit (SEN-truhl PROSS-ess-ing YOO-nit): the processor or part of the computer that processes software or information; sometimes called CPU

crashed (KRASHT): stopped working properly

cursor (KUR-sur): an indicator on your computer screen that shows your position when you're typing or pointing and clicking

digital (DIJ-uh-tuhl): using digits, or numbers

discs (DISKS): pieces of software containing information that can be inserted into a computer drive

electricity (i-lek-TRISS-uh-tee): a form of energy generated by the movement of electrons and protons

email (EE-mayl): short for electronic mail, sent over the Internet by one computer user to another

gigabyte (GIG-uh-bite): about a billion bytes

hard drives (HARD DRIVES): parts inside computers that store large amounts of information

Internet (IN-tur-net): an electronic web of billions of sites that you can connect to with a computer and modem

keyboard (KEE-bord): the board where you can type letters and numbers onto the computer screen

kilobyte (KIL-uh-bite): about a thousand bytes

mainframe (MAYN FRAYM): a large central computer that has memory and programs for smaller computers

megabyte (MEG-uh-bite): about a million bytes

memory (MEM-uh-ree): lets computers store and save files, information, and programs

modem (MOH-duhm): a computer output that connects the computer to the Internet

monitor (MON-uh-tur): the screen of a computer

mouse (MOUSS): a computer input that allows you to point and click to open programs or highlight things on the screen

PC (PEE-SEE): a personal computer that uses Microsoft software rather than a computer made by Apple

processor (PROSS-ess-ur): the part of the computer that handles all the information, sometimes called the central processing unit or CPU

RAM (RAM): stands for random access memory, the part of the computer's memory that is lost when the computer is turned off

reboot (re-BOOT): restart the computer

ROM (ROM): stands for read-only memory, the information that can be read but not changed

silicon chip (SIL-uh-kuhn CHIP): a computer chip that let computers get small enough for personal use

switches (SWICH-es): the devices that control the flow of binary signals

transistors (tran-ZISS-turz): devices that control the flow of electricity

websites (WEB-sites): a central location for related web pages on the Internet

Index

Further reading

Miller, Michael. *Absolute Beginner's Guide to Computer Basics (Fourth Edition)*. Que, 2007.

Reeves, Diane Lindsey. *Career Ideas for Kids Who Like Computers (Second Edition)*. Ferguson, 2007.

White, Ron and Downs, Timothy Edward. *How Computers Work (Ninth Edition)*. Que, 2007.

Websites

www.computerhope.com/
www.computerhelpatoz.com/
www.//library.thinkquest.org/5862/

About the Author

Don McLeese is a journalism professor at the University of Iowa. He has written many articles for newspapers and magazines and many books for young students as well.